CHRISTIAN MODESTY
AND THE
PUBLIC UNDRESSING OF AMERICA

Other Books From Vision Forum

Missionary Patriarch

How God Wants Us to Worship Him

Home-Making

Mother

Safely Home

The Bible Lessons of John Quincy Adams for His Son

The Letters and Lessons of Teddy Roosevelt for His Son

The Sinking of the Titanic

Of Plymouth Plantation

The Elsie Dinsmore Series

Cabin on the Prairie

Cabin in the Northwoods

Pollard's Child's History of America

Sergeant York and the Great War

The Life and Campaigns of Stonewall Jackson

The Boys' Guide to the
Historical Adventures of G.A. Henty

CHRISTIAN MODESTY
AND THE
PUBLIC UNDRESSING OF AMERICA

JEFF POLLARD

THE VISION FORUM, INC.
SAN ANTONIO, TEXAS

The Vision Forum, Inc.
4719 Blanco Rd.
San Antonio, Texas 78212
1-800-440-0022
www.visionforum.com

ISBN: 1-929241-34-8

Typography by Joshua R. Goforth
Cover Design by Darwin Pfingsten and Jeff Pollard

Printed in the United States of America

This is dedicated to my Lord and Savior Jesus Christ

his kingdom is an everlasting kingdom,
and his dominion is from generation to generation.

Daniel 4:3

and to my beloved wife, Myra

Strength and honour are her clothing . . .
. . . a woman that feareth the LORD, she shall be praised.

Proverbs 31:25, 31

TABLE OF CONTENTS

Publisher's Introduction

Dress Code and the Myth of Neutrality

By Douglas W. Phillips

Henry Van Til once observed that "culture is religion externalized." By this he meant that the culture of a nation reflects the true faith of that people. The way a people live their lives, they way they communicate, their philosophy of work, and their approach to aesthetics all reflect the standards and priorities of the people, and those priorities are dictated by their true faith.

This is why we must recognize that even dress is "religion externalized." Cultures that worship nature and treasure sensuality tend to dress immodestly. Those which make an idolatry out of material possessions, often fall prey to a foppish enslavement to high fashion. On the other hand, cultures which embrace true Christian piety will seek to make personal holiness the driving standard for their dress code. They will develop clothing which emphasizes biblical principles like distinction, functionality and modesty. In short, dress is not neutral.

Furthermore, dress standards and dress codes are inescapable and inevitable. Whether you realize it or not, you and everyone else have a dress code. You will either have a dress code by design (meaning that you have thought through the moral and philosophical implications of your dress code), or you will have a dress code by default (because you have let others do the thinking for you and have *de facto* accepted their conclusions), but you will have a dress code.

Until the 20th century, most Christians understood that dress standards were inescapable. But with the rise of antinomianism (the rejection of God as lawgiver), the resurgence of Gnosticism (the belief that God is not concerned with physical things) and the widespread acceptance of the neutrality postulate (the notion that the Lordship of Christ over human action only extends to "spiritual" matters), many 20th century Christians have simply allowed themselves to be swept away by cultural trends, rather than following the biblical admonition to take every thought and action captive to the obedience of Jesus Christ.

It must be clearly understood that every time you hear someone rant or rail that it is inherently "unfair" or "legalistic" to have rules pertaining to clothing, that such individuals are directly and unequivocally attacking the Lordship of Jesus Christ. Whether they realize it or not, they are in effect saying: "My dress standard is a neutral zone. Jesus does not speak to this issue."

Of course, it is entirely possible to be legalistic. The legalist is one who creates laws and rules foreign to Scripture by which he hopes to bind the consciences of men. Alternatively, he is that individual who teaches that one's entrance to Heaven is predicated on submission to a code of conduct. These teachings of the legalist are contra Scripture.

The real choice in the debate over standards of dress is not between legalism and license, but between God as lawgiver or man as lawgiver. Once that debate is settled, and the Lordship of Christ is freely and boldly proclaimed over our dress standards, then we can get about the business of studying the Scripture to discern how we can wisely apply the many diverse and relevant principles revealed in Scripture to the issue at hand.

Because the Bible teaches a doctrine the Reformers called "the sufficiency of Scripture" (namely, that God has given us in Scripture all we need for our faith and practice), we can be absolutely confident that the Bible is sufficient for us to know how we are to dress in a Christ-honoring manner relative to our culture, our gender, and our station in life.

Implicit to this notion is the idea that there may be an infinite number of God-honoring approaches to dress, relative to a specific culture, as well as an infinite number of Christ-dishonoring approaches to dress. The critical issue will be applying the unchanging principles, precepts, and normative patterns of Scripture to the ever changing facts of our cultural circumstances.

One of the most important of these issues to be addressed is the question of modesty and nakedness. The Bible has much to say on this issue. In fact, the Bible begins in Genesis 3 with the revelation that fallen man is to be covered, and that public nakedness is a sin. In past centuries, Christian peoples were often noted for their modesty, and heathen peoples for their immodesty. Today, the line between the professing Christian and the savage tribesman has become increasingly blurred, as more and more "Christian" people resort not only to the pagan practices of scarification, tattoos and body mutilation, but have thrown off the "restraints" of modest dress in favor of the trendy and the physically revealing. The result is that modern America has been publicly undressed. What is worse, Americans have come to think of nakedness as normal and acceptable, even preferable.

This brings me to the subject of the booklet in your hand, *The Public Undressing of America*. The author, Jeff Pollard, is a brave man. He has dared to tackle one of the great sacred cows of modern Christianity, and in so doing he has risked censure, disapproval and subjecting himself to the inevitable cries of "legalism." To this I retort, "Thanks be to God for raising up men who will speak the truth in love," which is exactly what Jeff does.

With winsome gentleness, but uncompromising boldness, Jeff Pollard helps modern Christians to understand the historic origins of our modern trend towards nakedness, and the implications of these trends on the people of America. This is a critical book for any parent who hopes to raise his sons and daughters to remain morally pure in a culture that worships the flesh.

I

MODESTY AND CONTROVERSY

And let us consider one another
to provoke unto love and to good works
Hebrews 10:24

Modesty is a controversial issue. No matter how the man of God approaches this subject, he will be judged a legalist or a libertarian by his audience. It's inescapable. Speaking against current fashion and popular trends is always difficult and costly for the man of God. Still, God has called him to a course that divinely steers him toward a head-on collision with the thinking and ways of the world. Vincent Alsop once said that a man must have "a very hardy spirit, that shall dare to cross the stream or stem the current of a prevailing luxuriancy. So that, to have a finger in this ungrateful debate, must engage him in Ishmael's fate,—to have every man's hand lifted up against him; seeing it is unavoidable, that his hand must be set almost against every man."[1] This certainly applies to the thorny issue of modesty. No doubt when we reach the end of this article, I will appear a spineless liberal to some; and to others I will be just another wave of legalism slapping upon the shores of Christian liberty.

My objective, however, is not controversy. I desire only to

---

[1] Vincent Alsop, *The Sinfulness of Strange Apparel*, in *Puritan Sermons 1659-1689 in Six Volumes*, Vol. III, (Wheaton, Illinois: Richard Owen Roberts, Publishers), 491.

glorify the Lord Jesus Christ and to provoke His people to love and good works (Heb 10:24). Nevertheless, since controversy is inevitable in this matter, I will follow this guideline: "[Love] will lend us one safe rule—that we impose a severer law upon ourselves, and allow a larger indulgence to others. The rule of our own conversation should be with the strictest; but that by which we censure others, a little more with the largest."[2]

While wrestling with a great controversy several hundred years ago, the great Samuel Bolton said, "My main aim is to convince the judgment not to irritate the affections, lest while I seek to be helpful to grace, I might render service to sin, and while I endeavor to lead men to holiness, I should stir up men's corruptions, and so run in vain. It is my earnest desire that what is here made obvious to the eye, the God of truth would make evident to the heart, and that He would give to my readers and myself sound judgment, that we may be able to distinguish between things that differ."[3]

This desire burns in my own heart! So then, love for Christ and His people is my motivation, and edification by God's truth is my goal. I beg the reader's forgiveness at whatever point that I fail to accomplish either of these. May the Lord Jesus Christ receive all the glory for whatever is right in this effort, and may His children receive whatever is profitable therein. All shortcomings in it are mine with my prayer for quick reproof for what errors it contains. Test it by the Scriptures; hold fast to that which is good. If you do not find the studies and conclusions here to be Biblical, reject them: Christ's free men should not be bound by the opinions of men. And if you find them to be in harmony with God's Word, bow to His truth and serve Him with joy and gladness.

---

[2] Ibid.

[3] Samuel Bolton, *The True Bounds of Christian Freedom*, (Edinburgh: The Banner of Truth Trust, 1978), 14.

II
DEFINING TERMS

*In like manner also, that women adorn themselves in modest
apparel, with shamefacedness and sobriety . . . 1 Timothy 2:9*

As a new believer, I attended an annual youth conference at a
beach in Florida. Several questions about the propriety of the
states of dress and undress at the conference drove me to God's
Word and prayer, and these led me to conclude that I would no
longer attend that meeting. I also had children who were asking
me honest questions about these matters. My attempts to explain
to the founder of the conference *why* I would no longer attend
and to answer my children's questions resulted in this study.

Regarding the conference: my concerns were not the
orthodoxy nor the abilities of the teachers who led it. All that
was fine. They, as well as I, firmly declared that they believed in
the Lordship of Jesus Christ in every area of the Christian's life;
likewise the doctrine of Christian liberty. What troubled me,
however, was this: the beach with its accompanying lascivious
atmosphere coupled with the dress of the conference attendees
did not seem in harmony with the preaching of God's holiness.
This produced a confusing message, a conflicting mixture of
holiness and impurity. It reminded me of the stale smell of
perfume mixed with cigarette smoke.

This led me to examine modesty in *general* and then
swimwear in *particular*. Why swimwear? Because Scriptural

evidence convinced me that modern swimwear is immodest nakedness; and historical evidence convinced me that it was *designed* to be so. After a good bit of research I discovered that the fashion industry employed swimwear to change public opinion about modesty. In other words, fashion designers *used* swimwear to *undress* America. And this is diametrically opposed to Christian modesty. Examining the issues regarding swimwear will, I hope, instruct us in the larger arenas of fashion and modesty.

So then, what *is* modesty? Like the words *love* and *faith*, we often use the word *modesty* without grasping its real meaning. Modern dictionaries offer definitions like these:

1. Having or showing a moderate estimation of one's own talents, abilities, and value.

2. Having or proceeding from a disinclination to call attention to oneself; retiring or diffident.

3. Reserve or propriety in speech, dress, or behavior.

4. Free from showiness or ostentation; unpretentious.

5. Moderate or limited in size, quantity, or range; not extreme: a *modest* price; a newspaper with a *modest* circulation.[4]

Noah Webster defines *modesty* as "That lowly temper which accompanies a moderate estimate of one's own worth and importance." He adds, "In females, modesty has the like character as in males; but the word is used also as synonymous with chastity, or purity of manners. In this sense, modesty results from purity of mind, or from the fear of disgrace and ignominy fortified by education and principle. Unaffected modesty is the sweetest charm of female excellence, the richest gem in the diadem of their honor."[5]

---

[4] *The American Heritage® Dictionary of the English Language*, Third Edition copyright © 1992 by Houghton Mifflin Company.

[5] Noah Webster, *American Dictionary of the English Language*, 1828 5th ed. (G. & C. Merriam Company; reprint ed., San Francisco, California: Foundation for American Christian Education, 1987).

According to these definitions then, modesty is a broad concept not limited to sexual connotation. It's a state of mind or disposition that expresses a humble estimate of one's self before God. Modesty, like humility, is the opposite of boldness or arrogance. It doesn't seek to draw attention to itself or to show off in an unseemly way. Webster apparently links chastity with modesty because chastity means moral purity in thought and conduct. Moral purity, like humility, will not exhibit sensuality any more than ostentation.

Several words shed light on a Biblical view of modesty. 1Timothy 2:9 says that women should "adorn themselves in modest apparel, with shamefacedness and sobriety." The word translated *modest*[6] has "the general meaning of 'respectable,' 'honorable,' and when used in reference to women means elsewhere, as here, 'modest'."[7] George Knight III notes that "adornment and dress is an area with which women are often concerned and in which there are dangers of immodesty or indiscretion." So "Paul makes that the focal point of his warning and commands women 'to adorn themselves' in keeping with their Christian profession and life."[8] Hence, modesty is an element of Christian character, and our dress should make the same "profession" that we do. Paul's directive implies that this is an especially dangerous matter for women.

According to Knight, *shamefacedness*[9] denotes "a state of mind or attitude necessary for one to be concerned about modesty and thus to dress modestly."[10] It means "a moral feeling, *reverence, awe, respect* for the feeling or opinion of others or for one's own conscience and so *shame, self-respect . . . sense of*

---

6 κόσμιος {kos'-mee-os}.

7 George W. Knight, III, *New International Greek Testament Commentary, Commentary on the Pastoral Epistles*, (Grand Rapids, Michigan: W.B. Eerdmans Publishing Co., 1992) , 133.

8 Ibid.

9 αἰδώς {ahee-doce'}.

10 Knight, *Pastoral Epistles*, 134.

honor." William Hendriksen says it "indicates a *sense of shame*, a shrinking from trespassing the boundaries of propriety."[11] This means that modesty knows the boundaries and desires to stay within them—it doesn't desire to show off.

Finally, *sobriety* has among its meanings "the general one of 'good judgment, moderation, self-control,' which when seen as 'a feminine virtue' is understood as 'decency, chastity.'"[12] *Sobriety* signifies "a command over bodily passions, a state of self-mastery in the area of the appetite. The basic meaning of the word has different nuances and connotations and represents 'that habitual inner self-government, with its constant rein on all the passions and desires, which would hinder the temptation to [immodesty] from arising' . . . in effect, Paul is saying that when such attitudes self-consciously control a woman's mind, the result is evident in her modest apparel."[13] Kelly says of *shamefacedness* and *sobriety*, "the former, used only here in the N.T., connotes feminine reserve in matters of sex. The latter . . . basically stands for perfect self-mastery in the physical appetites . . . As applied to women it too had a definitely sexual nuance."[14]

I've taken the time to unfold these words a bit because there are ministers today who take Paul's words as applying *only* to luxurious, expensive, or gaudy clothing in church. Their point is that such clothing would "distract" in the worship services. However, they want to stop there and go no further. I wholeheartedly agree that this idea is included, but these men overlook or ignore the sexual aspect that is *clearly* in Paul's mind. "While his remarks conform broadly to the conventional diatribe against female extravagance, what is probably foremost in his mind is the impropriety of women exploiting their physical charms on such occasions, and also the emotional disturbance they are liable to

[11] William Hendriksen, *New Testament Commentary, Thessalonians, Timothy, Titus*, (Grand Rapids, Mich.: Baker Book House, 1979), 106.

[12] Knight, *Pastoral Epistles*, 134.

[13] Ibid.

[14] J. N. D. Kelly, *The Pastoral Epistles*, (Peabody, Massachusetts: Hendrickson Publishers, 1960), 66.

cause their male fellow-worshipers."[15] Knight explains that "the reason for Paul's prohibition of elaborate hair styles, ornate jewelry, and extremely expensive clothing becomes clear when one reads in the contemporary literature of the inordinate time, expense, and effort that elaborately braided hair and jewels demanded, not just as ostentatious display, but also as the mode of dress of courtesans and harlots . . . it is the excess and sensuality that Paul forbids."[16]

Excess *and* sensuality—both of these bear on modesty. Christian women must self-consciously control their hearts and passions, instead of arraying themselves elaborately, expensively, and/or sensuously. If they are modest, they will not draw attention to themselves in the wrong way. Their dress will not say "SEX!" or "PRIDE!" or "MONEY!", but *"purity," "humility,"* and *"moderation."*

One more point: because the immediate context of Paul's epistle to Timothy regards the Christian's behavior in church, there are those who claim that Paul limits his discussion to distractions in church, not principles of dress at all times. Again, I believe this entirely misses Paul's point. The church is "the pillar and ground of the truth" (1 Tim 3:15). Therefore, the principles we are taught for ordering our lives in the worship of God should ultimately guide our daily living in the presence of God. Can one honestly conclude that a woman should dress modestly in the presence of men and God for corporate worship only to dress pridefully and sensuously outside of church meetings? Knight's insight is keen here: "Therefore, Paul's instructions to women, like the preceding instructions to men, are related to the context of the gathered Christian community but are not restricted to it. Men must always live holy lives that avoid wrath and dispute, particularly in connection with prayer for others; women are always to live in accord with their profession of godliness, dressing modestly and discreetly, and manifesting a proper relationship to men as regards the

---

[15] Ibid.

[16] Knight, *Pastoral Epistles*, 135.

question of authority."[17] We have then a Biblical directive for modest apparel that begins in the context of our corporate worship and that extends from there to our daily living.

However, having said that, modesty is not *first* an issue of clothing. It is primarily *an issue of the heart*. And if the heart is right with God, it will govern itself in purity coupled with humility and will express itself modestly. Calvin observes, "Yet we must always begin with the dispositions; for where debauchery reigns within, there will be no chastity; and where ambition reigns within, there will be no modesty in the outward dress." [18] He concludes, "Undoubtedly the dress of a virtuous and godly woman must differ from that of a strumpet . . . if piety must be testified by works, this profession ought also to be visible in chaste and becoming dress."[19] Again, this applies not only to corporate worship, but to daily living. Though it is true that one may dress modestly from a sinful and prideful motive, one cannot *knowingly* dress lavishly and sensually from a good one. Thus, the purity and humility of a regenerate heart *internally* must ultimately express itself by modest clothing *externally*.

Therefore, since *modesty* has several definitions, we will draw ours from the Biblical material: Christian modesty is the inner self-government, rooted in a proper understanding of one's self before God, which outwardly displays itself in humility and purity from a genuine love for Jesus Christ, rather than in self-glorification or self-advertisement. Christian modesty then will not publicly expose itself in sinful *nakedness*.

---

[17] Ibid, 131.

[18] John Calvin, *Calvin's Commentaries* Vol. XXI, "The First Epistle to Timothy," (Edinburgh, Scotland: Calvin Translation Society; reprint ed., Grand Rapids, Michigan: Baker Book House Company, 1993), 66.

[19] Ibid.

III

GOD, THE DESIGNER OF CLOTHES

Unto Adam also and to his wife did the LORD God
make coats of skins, and clothed them.
Genesis 3:21

Those of us who profess to be born of God's Spirit agree that we must reject *sinful nakedness* and practice *modesty*. But does the Bible offer an objective standard for each? I believe it does. The difficulty lies in defining these terms with Biblical accuracy instead of personal opinion. Scripture identifies God as Sovereign Creator of all things, as well as the Originator and Designer of clothing. The Biblical account of the origin of clothing and its subsequent examples of dress reveal at least one simple maxim: God designed clothing to cover the *body*, not just the private parts. [Please note: this is *not* an argument for a return to the *mode* of dress worn in Biblical times. The examples cited only suggest the *purpose* and *function* of clothing and the *approximate area* of the body that clothes were designed to cover.]

I. *When There Were No Clothes*. Genesis 2:25 says, "And they were both naked, the man and his wife, and were not ashamed." It's important to understand that in the beginning, nakedness was *not* shameful. In fact, "God saw every thing that he had made, and, behold, it was very good" (Gen 1:31). Though Adam and Eve were naked, they felt no sense of public disgrace or humiliation; their nakedness was very *good* because God created them that way. Under these circumstances clothing was unnecessary. So what transformed *good* nakedness into something *shameful*? And why did God Himself *cover* man's body? Consider carefully the following answers.

II. *When God Gave Clothes*. Nakedness was good until Adam and Eve rebelled against God. At that point sin entered and shame followed: "And the eyes of them both were opened, and they knew that they *were* naked; and they sewed fig leaves together, and made themselves aprons . . . And he said, I heard thy voice in the garden, and I was afraid because I *was* naked and I hid myself . . . Unto Adam also and to his wife did the LORD God make coats of skins, and clothed them" (Gen 3:7, 10, 21). As a result of their fall into sin, God *covered* Adam and Eve's nakedness. The knowledge of their sin transformed their experience of "good" nakedness into stinging, humiliating shame. Blushing and disgrace entered history, but thankfully the story doesn't end there. In His great mercy God provided a *gracious covering*.

The main point of this account is its spiritual or *Gospel* application: Adam and Eve lost their righteous standing with God and were "naked" in their sin. God then killed animals and fashioned coats of skins to graciously "cover" Adam and Eve after they pitifully attempted to cover themselves with "aprons" of their own works. This beautiful *type* of God's mercy and grace was later fulfilled in the propitiatory sacrifice of Jesus Christ. Thomas Boston comments,

> But on surer grounds we may observe, that our first parents made their first garments, and God made the next, which were effectual for the use of garments. Whence we may learn the utter insufficiency of our own righteousness to cover spiritual nakedness, and the absolute necessity of the righteousness of God, the imputed righteousness, with its fitness every way to clothe the sinful soul.[20]

---

[20] Thomas Boston, *Of the Origins, Names, Texture and Use of Garments*, in *The Complete Works of Thomas Boston*, ed. by Samuel M'Millan, VI (Wheaton: Richard Owen Roberts, Publishers, 1980), 239.

God used this *literal* event to teach us a *spiritual* truth. He replaced Adam and Eve's loincloths[21] with "tunics of skin."[22] Although Adam covered his loins, God covered him from his neck to his knees. This is not insignificant: the work of Adam's hands was not acceptable to God either spiritually (his works righteousness) or physically (his nakedness); only the covering that God Himself provided was sufficient for both. While Adam covered his privates, the Lord covered Adam's *body*. Alsop observed that "our first parents, in that hasty provision which they made against their shame, took care only for aprons: but God—who had adequate conceptions of their wants, and what was necessary to supply them; of the rule of decency, and what would fully answer it—provided for them coats; that so the whole body . . . might be covered, and concealed."[23]

Though we have no "snapshots" of Adam and Eve's apparel, the word *coats* is consistently used throughout the O.T. to mean a tunic-like garment. *Coats* in Gen 3:21 is *kuttōnet*[24] from an unused root meaning *to cover*. The *kuttōnet* was the ordinary garment worn by man and woman as seen in the tunics of skin worn by Adam and Eve.[25] This shirt-like garment usually had long sleeves, and extended down to the ankles when worn as a dress coat. "Hard-working men, slaves, and prisoners wore them more abbreviated — sometimes even to their knees, and without sleeves —."[26] Several well known lexicons echo that it

---

[20] Thomas Boston, *Of the Origins, Names, Texture and Use of Garments*, in *The Complete Works of Thomas Boston*, ed. by Samuel M'Millan, VI (Wheaton: Richard Owen Roberts, Publishers, 1980), 239.

[21] חֲגוֹר, {khag-ore'} *girdle, loin-covering, belt, loin-cloth, armour.*

[22] Gordon Wenham, *Word Biblical Commentary: Vol 1, Genesis 1-15*, (Waco, Texas: Word Books, Publisher, 1987), 84.

[23] Alsop, *Sinfulness*, 494.

[24] כְּתֹנֶת {keth-o'-neth } or כֻּתֹּנֶת {koot-to'-neth}

[25] *Zondervan Pictorial Encyclopedia of the Bible*, Vol.2, s.v. "Dress," by W. H.. Mare.

[26] *Zondervan Pictorial Bible Dictionary*, s.v. "Dress," by G. Frederick Owen and Steven Barabas.

was "[the] principal ordinary garment of man and woman, worn next to the skin[27] . . . a long shirt-like garment usually of linen[28] . . . Adam's was made of fur."[29] The *kuttōnet* resembled the Roman 'tunic' corresponding most nearly to our 'long shirt,' reaching below the knees always, and, in case it was designed for dress occasions, reaching almost to the ground;[30] while the simplest kind was sleeveless, reaching only to the knees.[31] Another description tells us that it was made of linen or wool and reached down to the knees or to the ankles.[32] All these sources agree regarding the *kuttōnet*: it covered the body from at least the neck to the knees, while sometimes reaching mid-calf or all the way to the feet.

The important thing to remember is that this was *God's* design for *covering* Adam and Eve's nakedness and shame. In other words, God did *not* give a fur bikini to represent our righteousness and salvation. Moreover, this was not the only time God used this design.

III. *When God Gave the Priesthood Clothes.* God not only ordained the priests to their holy office, He designed their holy garb as well. He said to Moses, "And thou shalt speak unto all *that are* wise hearted, whom I have filled with the spirit of wisdom, that they may make Aaron's garments to consecrate him, that he may minister unto me in the priest's office. And these *are* the garments which they shall make: a breastplate, and an ephod, and a robe, and a broidered coat (*kuttōnet*), a mitre, and a girdle: and they shall make holy garments for Aaron thy brother, and his sons, that he may minister unto me in the

---

[27] *The New Brown-Driver-Briggs-Gesenius Hebrew-English Lexicon*, (Peabody, Massachusetts: Hendrickson Publishers, 1979).

[28] James Strong, *Exhaustive Concordance of the Bible*, (Nashville: Abingdon, 1890).

[29] *Theological Wordbook of the Old Testament*, Vol 1, s.v. "Kuttōnet" by Gleason J. Archer, Jr.

[30] *The International Standard Bible Encyclopaedia*, Vol. 2 , s.v. "Dress," by George B. Eager.

[31] *Wycliffe Bible Encyclopedia*, Vol. 1, s.v. "Dress" by Edgar C. James.

[32] *New Bible Dictionary*, s.v. "Dress," by C. de Wit.

priest's office" (Exo 28.3,4). So God, the Original Designer of Clothing, covered their bodies as He had Adam and Eve's.

IV. *When God Wore Clothes*. The Lord Jesus Christ is the Word Who became flesh and dwelt among us (Joh 1:14). A fair question then would be, "When God became man, what did *He* wear?" The answer to this is worthy of this lengthy quote from Alfred Edersheim:

> Three, or else four articles commonly constituted the dress of the body. First came the undergarment, commonly the *Chaluq* or the *Kittuna* (the Biblical *Kethoneth*), from which later some have derived the word 'cotton.' The *Chaluq* might be of linen or of wool. The sages wore it down to the feet. It was covered by the upper garment or *Tallith* to within about a handbreadth. The *Chaluq* lay close to the body, and had no other opening than that round the neck and for the arms. At the bottom it had a kind of hem. To possess only one such 'coat' or inner garment was a mark of poverty. Hence, when the Apostles were sent on their temporary mission, they were directed not to take 'two coats.' Closely similar to, if not identical with, the *Chaluq*, was the ancient garment mentioned in the Old Testament as *Kethoneth* to which the Greek '*Chiton*' corresponds. As the garment which our Lord wore, and those of which He spoke to His Apostles are designated by that name, we conclude that it represents the well-known *Kethoneth* or Rabbinic *Kittuna*. This might be of almost any material, even leather, though it was generally of wool or flax . . . We can now form an approximate idea of the outward appearance of Jesus on that spring-morning amidst the throng at Capernaum. He would, we may safely assume, go about in the ordinary, although not in the more ostentatious, dress, worn by the Jewish teachers of Galilee . . . The *Chaluq*, or more probably the *Kittuna*, which formed His inner garment, must have been close-fitting, and descended to His feet. Since it was not only so worn by teachers,

but was, regarded as absolutely necessary for any one who could publicly read or 'Targum' the Scriptures, or exercise any function in the Synagogue.[33]

So our Lord Jesus Christ, the Living God come in the flesh, *covered* Himself in the same way that He had covered Adam and Eve and the holy priesthood. Is Christ a good example for us?

V. *When God Gives the Saints in Heaven Clothes.* The Apostle John gives us a vision of the saints in heaven: "And white robes were given unto every one of them; and it was said unto them, that they should rest yet for a little season, until their fellowservants also and their brethren, that should be killed as they were, should be fulfilled" (Rev 6:11; 7:9, 13, 14). This robe[34] is a loose, outer garment for men extending to the feet, worn by kings, priests, and persons of rank. The lexicons identify this as either a "long, flowing robe"[35] or the "long and flowing upper garment, and sometimes the special robe of priests . . ."[36]

It appears then that the Bible *does* offer us a standard for *covering* the body. From the coats God gave to Adam to the robes He designed for the priests and from the garments of Jesus Christ to the clean, white robes of the saints in glory, we have a consistent testimony. The Old and New Testaments reveal that God's earthly and heavenly people wore garments that covered them from at least the neck-to-below the knee (possibly mid-calf to ankle). These passages coupled with others indicate that Christians have a standard for *covering* their bodies, especially when they gather corporately to worship the living God.

---

[33] Alfred Edersheim, *Life and Times of Jesus the Messiah*, (New York: Longmans, Green, and Co., 1904), 622, 624.

[34] στολη {stol-ay}.

[35] Walter Bauer, F. Wilbur Gingrich, and Frederick W. Danker, *A Greek-English Lexicon of the New Testament and Other Early Christian Literature*, 5th ed, (Chicago: University of Chicago Press, 1979).

[36] Gerhard Kittel and Gerhard Friedrich, Editors, *The Theological Dictionary of the New Testament*, Abridged in One Volume (Grand Rapids, Michigan: W.B. Eerdmans Publishing Co., 1985), s.v., *stolē*, " by U. Wilckens.

Calvin comments that "since dress is an indifferent matter, (as all outward matters are) it is difficult to assign a fixed limit, how far we ought to go . . . This at least will be settled beyond all controversy, that every thing in dress which is not in accordance with modesty and sobriety must be disapproved."[37] Calvin is correct: it *is* difficult to assign a fixed limit. However, since God Himself covered Adam and the priests; and since Christ covered Himself as He covers the saints in heaven, don't we have a perfect standard for modesty and sobriety? When we believers do not have a black and white command in the Bible, our normal practice is to search God's perfect record for a principle from which we may draw a proper conclusion. If we reject this practice, where *will* we find a standard of modesty? Whatever else may be drawn from these Scriptural accounts, it is obvious that clothes *covered* the body, especially in worship. Let me emphasize again, my argument is *not* for a return to robe-like garments: I'm arguing for the *function* of clothing in its relation to modesty. Adam, the Priesthood, Jesus Christ, and the glorified saints all point to one clear fact: God's people should be *covered*. And the Biblical model suggests a standard of at least neck-to-below the knee.

[37] Calvin, *Commentaries* Vol. XXI, 66.

IV

DEFINING THE ISSUE: NAKEDNESS AND SHAME

I counsel thee to buy of me . . . white raiment, that thou mayest be clothed, and that the shame of thy nakedness do not appear.
Revelation 3:18

As evidenced by the *Song of Solomon* and numerous other portions of Scripture, sexual attraction and sexual relations between man and wife are neither shameful nor sinful. However, after Adam's fall, *nakedness* became a biblical euphemism for male and female reproductive organs and is most often associated with shame. It also regards sinful or shameful sexual acts.

"None of you shall approach to any that is near of kin to him, to uncover *their* nakedness: I *am* the LORD. The nakedness of thy father, or the nakedness of thy mother, shalt thou not uncover: she *is* thy mother; thou shalt not uncover her nakedness" (Lev 18:6,7; see also v. 11-18).

"And if a man shall lie with a woman having her sickness, and shall uncover her nakedness . . . both of them shall be cut off from among their people" (Lev 20:18).

To "uncover nakedness" means to commit sinful, sexual acts. Here there can be no argument: according to God's Word, uncovering someone's nakedness for the purpose of unlawful sexual relations is sinful and shameful. Obviously, these are secret or private acts—what about *public displays* of nakedness?

The words translated *nakedness*, which specifically refer to the private parts in both Hebrew and Greek, are most frequently associated with *shame*. Here are just a few examples: "Thy nakedness shall be uncovered, yea, thy shame shall be seen."[38] "Behold, therefore I will gather all thy lovers, with whom thou hast taken pleasure, and all *them* that thou hast loved, with all *them* that thou hast hated; I will even gather them round about against thee, and will discover thy nakedness unto them, that they may see all thy nakedness."[39] "Behold, I *am* against thee, saith the LORD of hosts; and I will discover thy skirts upon thy face, and I will shew the nations thy nakedness, and the kingdoms thy shame."[40] "I counsel thee to buy of me gold tried in the fire, that thou mayest be rich; and white raiment, that thou mayest be clothed, and *that* the shame of thy nakedness do not appear; and anoint thine eyes with eyesalve, that thou mayest see."[41] These passages clearly teach that the public exposure of one's private parts is associated with shame.

However, *nakedness* is not limited to exposing the privates. When a man took off his *kuttōnet*, he was in a state the Bible calls *naked* (*gumnos*). While still dressed in his undergarment, Peter was "naked" in John 21:7, because he had taken off his outer garment.[42] Burton Scott Easton says, "Both the Gr and Heb forms mean 'without clothing,' but in both languages they are used frequently in the sense of 'lightly clad' or, simply, 'without an outer garment.'" Thomas Boston observed that "the Hebrews call him naked who hath cast off his upper garment."[43]

---

[38] Isaiah 47:3a; Nah 3:5.

[39] Ezekiel 16:37.

[40] Nahum 3:5.

[41] Revelation 3:18.

[42] ἐπενδύτης {ep-en-doo'-tace} •from 1902; n m • AV - fisher's coat 1; 1 • 1) an upper garment 1a) John 21:7 seems to denote a kind of linen blouse or frock which fishermen used to wear at their work.

[43] Boston, *Garments*, 237.

So, probably, is the meaning in John 21:7—"Peter was wearing only the *chiton*."[44] Peter was not *sinfully* naked in the context of his work: as a fisherman he was *laboring* among men away from shore, not publicly *socializing* in a mixed gathering. Nevertheless, he obviously saw a difference between working in his boat and being on shore in the presence of His Lord, because he *covered* himself and then swam to Christ. Why? Because he was "naked."

So then, according to Scripture, one doesn't have to be *stark* naked to be *shamefully* naked. *Gumnos* means "naked, stripped bare; and without an outer garment, without which a decent person did not appear in public."[45] This second kind of nakedness not only applies to Peter in John 21, but to the prophet Isaiah[46] and King Saul.[47] Peter's undergarment actually covered more of his body than would most modern shorts or swimwear for men! Though this was not *necessarily* sinful, it was associated with public shame as Arndt-Gingrich's definition implies. A decent person did not appear in public this way. This is why Peter put on his outer garment before swimming to shore and why Isaiah was a sign of shame, disgrace, and Judgment to Egypt and Cush. The same could be said for the humiliation of the "Virgin daughter of Babylon" (Isa 47:1-3) in her "making bare the leg and uncovering the thigh."[48] Isaiah's "nakedness" would not even be noticed at your average Christian retreat today. Making bare the leg and uncovering the thigh are not only viewed as "normal" practice today, they are considered one's liberty.

Moreover, public *nakedness* went hand in hand with ancient pagan religion. Fashion expert Alison Lurie notes, "Historically

---

[44] *International Standard Bible Encyclopaedia* Vol III, s.v. "Naked," by Burton Scott Easton.

[45] Bauer, *A Greek-English Lexicon.*

[46] Isaiah 20:1-6.

[47] 1 Samuel 19:24.

[48] See commentaries on Isaiah by Young, Alexander, Delitzsch, Leupold, Lange, Gill, and Henry.

. . . shame seems to have played very little part in development of costume. In ancient Egypt, Crete, and Greece, the naked body was not considered immodest; slaves and athletes habitually went without clothing, while people of high rank wore garments that were cut and draped so as to show a good deal when in motion."[49] So while a naked body was not uncommon for paganism, being without one's outer garment was considered *immodest* and even shameful among God's people. God's people *cover* their bodies in public, while pagans often *uncover* theirs.

Nakedness also goes hand in hand with demon possession: "And when he went forth to land, there met him out of the city a certain man, which had devils long time, and ware no clothes . . . Then they went out to see what was done; and came to Jesus, and found the man, out of whom the devils were departed, sitting at the feet of Jesus, clothed, and in his right mind . . ." (Luke 8:26-35). When driven by the devils, the demoniac was *naked*; when in his right mind by the power and grace of Jesus Christ, he was *covered*. As we have seen, God covered man in the Garden; it appears that Satan and the devils have been trying to strip him ever since. And quite successfully.

Clearly then, some forms of public nakedness are shameful and/or explicitly sinful since the Fall of Adam. Exposing the male or female body, which should be *covered*, is out of harmony with the Biblical model. Moreover, since exposing the privates is shameful, it seems obvious that clothing which emphasizes or purposely draws attention to these areas of the body is likewise shameful and immodest. And modern swimwear is the epitome of these things—by *design*.

---

[49] Alison Lurie, *The Language of Clothes*, (New York: Random House, 1981), 212-214.

V

The Public Undressing of America

. . . and the woman was very beautiful to look upon.
2 Samuel 11:2

Swimwear in American culture does not possess a dark and mysterious origin buried somewhere in the annals of fashion antiquity. A trip to the public library and several hours of research will unfold a provocative and revealing story. The rise and progress of swimwear in our culture reveals not only a great deal of flesh, but also a great deal about our society. Kidwell and Steele observe that "the history of swimwear is connected to our changing perceptions of modesty and immodesty. Throughout its history, the swimsuit has typically been the most revealing form of sportswear and it has forced an uneasy alliance between modesty and sexual display."[50] Several works of fashion history specifically chronicle this "uneasy alliance." I have quoted them freely so that I will not be accused of "inventing" this story to make my point. These books are not written from a Christian perspective. Hardly. They did not seep out of the fevered brain of some mean-spirited, fundamentalist preacher. And this is what makes them valuable: they *don't* tell the story from the viewpoint of Christian modesty. My desire is to let *them* speak in their own words, for it is *their* testimony that the swimsuit was the primary

---

[50] Claudia Brush Kidwell and Valerie Steele, *Men and Women: Dressing the Part*, (Washington: Smithsonian Institute Press, 1989), 118.

player in the undressing of America. In fact, the histories of swimwear and fashion generally present the story of how America undressed as a *good* one, a liberating one. I find it a sad one.

Bathing costumes can be traced to around 350 B.C. in Greece and later to Rome where bathing and swimming reached the peak of their popularity. A mural found in Sicily's Piazza Armerina pictures young maidens wearing scanty garments that are dead ringers for modern bikinis. However, water sports went out of style after the fall of the Empire and did not reappear until the early 1700s in French and English spas. The attire was a toga-like garment for both men and women. Later in the early 1800s, going to the beach for recreation began to catch on in America; but all the water activities were strictly segregated with each sex either on its own secluded stretch of beach or alternating in springs or pools at different hours. When fashionable sea resorts became popular, so did swimming and sunbathing. However, aside from these toga-like garments, no real prototypes for bathing attire seem to have existed throughout history. Hence, the rise in popularity of swimming and sunbathing presented a new challenge to the world of fashion.

And what was this *new* challenge? First was the new situation of men and women frolicking *together* in mixed water sports. Prior to this men and women swam nude or with little on in *segregated* groups. Though there have been some exceptions to this, segregation was the general practice.

Into this new atmosphere of men and women together in the water, a great need for a *new* garment arose. This garment would have to be functional in a way that streetwear could not be. Street clothes became heavy when saturated with water and even dangerous. However, because the new garment had to be less bulky to allow greater freedom of movement, it became more and more abbreviated for both sexes. This truly *was* something new: more and more men and women together with less and less on their bodies.

Here lay the heart of the challenge: with men and women

freely swimming and playing together in the water, there had to be a garment that would liberate the body for movement. Yet woven into the fabric of our society were the vestiges of a Biblically-influenced modesty. The Christian perspective emanated from the Scriptural account that God gave garments to *cover* the body, but the demand for greater body movement required this new garment to *uncover* the body. Fashion designers understood that this seaworthy apparel would have to *conceal*, yet they well knew that to give its wearers liberty of movement, it would by its very nature *reveal*. "This amphibious costume would have to be something of a sartorial paradox, a form of undress that functioned as a symbol of dress."[51] Once men and women were no longer segregated in their seaside activities, an inevitable aquatic striptease began. The remaining attempts to retain some trace of modesty and yet liberate the arms and legs explains why early swimwear had the awkward and bulky appearance that our culture presently finds so amusing. Nevertheless, we must not miss this point: these early, funny looking swimsuits were, at least for a time, an attempt to continue the time honored, Christian ideal of *covering* the body.

Swimwear designers wrestled with a perplexing problem: swimwear had to function in the waves *and* on the beach, from the dressing room to the water's edge. The standards of modesty at that time clearly demanded *concealment*, yet functionality in the water demanded *abbreviation*. And given the fact that the fashion industry was not generally guided by God's Word, nothing but the old-fashioned view of modesty stood in the way of exposing more and more of the body. What the evidence reveals and what we must bear in mind is that the streamlining and deletions in swimwear were clearly *by design*.

Here we must pause and reflect on this fact: what was taking place on the beach was the beginning in modern times of the violent clash between *the Holy God* as the designer of clothes

---

[51] Lena Lenček and Gideon Bosker, *Making Waves: Swimsuits and the Undressing of America* (San Francisco, California: Chronicle Books, 1989), 11.

and *sinful men* as the designer of clothes.

Fashion designers did not view swimwear as simply functional garments with a specific use like overalls. They envisioned their creations as highly *fashionable* garments, and therefore designed them both to *reveal* and *arouse*. What they clearly understood is that this new aquatic garment was merely a *symbol* of dress. This is why swimwear ultimately evolved into a form of nakedness thinly disguised as dress. Moreover, they were aware that they were undressing the American public and constantly challenged the legal limits of public nakedness. I challenge you, dear reader: read the books penned by the fashion industry; read their histories of the trade; you will discover that fashion's guiding perspective is often sexual attraction, not the Word of God. And this is an underlying theme in this article: instead of being guided by God's Word, the voice from heaven, American culture is driven by Fashion, the voice of fallen men.

Here it will be instructive to examine the influence of Europe on our society, especially that of France. Although the American colonies were founded upon the Gospel of Jesus Christ, they gradually drifted away from God's word and then from the holiness and modesty which the Gospel promotes. How did this happen?

The 1800s proved to be a most turbulent time in our once Christian nation (I'm not implying that everyone *was* a Christian, for this certainly wasn't the case. Nevertheless, the American colonies had inherited and were growing up in a *world and life view* that was generally Christian. This was clearly reflected in many of America's laws.). During that period the cracks in the dam of our waning morality began to give way to the pressure of European style, philosophy, political thought, and theology. This phenomenon was not new: the great preachers John Owen and Thomas Brooks both chronicled a similar decline in England at an earlier period and roundly condemned the corrupting influence of European fashion!

Hereunto of late have been added vanity in apparel,

with foolish, light, lascivious modes and dressings therein, and an immodest boldness in *behavior*[52] among men and women. These corruptions, which, being borrowed from the neighbour nation . . . have brought forth the fruit of vanity and pride in abundance. And it is the most manifest evidence of a degenerate people, when they are prone to *naturalize the vices* of other nations among them . . .[53]

But you will say, What sins were there among the professing people in London . . . ?

Ans. I answer, That there were these seven sins, among others, to be found amongst many of them . . . [1.] First, There was among many professors of the gospel in London *too great a conformity to the fashions of the world.* How many professing men in that great city were dressed up like fantastical buffoons,[54] and women like Bartholomew-babies,[55] to the dishonour of God, the shame of religion, the hardening of the wicked, the grieving of the weak, and the provoking of divine justice! . . . [Zephaniah 1:8] is a stinging and flaming check against all fashion-mongers, against all such as seem to have consulted with French, Italian, Persian, and all outlandish monsters, to advise them of all their several modes and fashions of vice, and that are so dexterous at following of them, that they are more complete in them than their pattern. Certainly, if ever such wantons be saved, it will be by fire. Strange

---

[52] Owen's original word is *conversation*.

[53] John Owen, *The Nature and Causes of Apostasy*, in *The Works of John Owen*, W. H. Goold ed. Vol. VII (Johnstone & Hunter 1850-53; reprint ed., Edinburgh, Scotland: The Banner of Truth Trust), 207.

[54] Brooks' original word was *antics*, which means buffoon or one that practices odd gesticulations.

[55] These were *dolls sold at Bartholomew Fair*. They were flashy, bespangled dolls offered at the fair, which celebrated at the Feast of St. Bartholomew. A national and international event, it was a spectacular display of musicians, acrobats, freaks, wild animals, side-shows, and the like.

apparel is part of the old man, that must be put off, if ever men or women intend to go to heaven . . . Cyrian and Augustine draw up this conclusion: that superfluous apparel is worse than whoredom, because whoredom only corrupts chastity, but this corrupts nature . . . O sirs! What was more common among many professors in London than to be clothed in strange apparel, *a la mode de France*?[56]

Though the Word of God commands, "And be not conformed to this world: but be ye transformed by the renewing of your mind, that ye may prove what *is* that good, and acceptable, and perfect, will of God,"[57] the American fashion industry began to ape European fashion.

Swimwear manufacturers knew *exactly* the course they planned to follow, and it wasn't the Word of God: ". . . in part thanks to the influence of the more daringly cut French swimsuits, the American bathing costume underwent a revolution. Until that time, bathing attire had been modeled on streetwear . . . by the 1890s, however, underwear began a relentless if slow migration outward that would come to a full, triumphal exposure in the bikini of the 1960s."[58] It should be no surprise then for us to learn that "what the conceivers of the suit strove to suppress was the natural association between underwear and swimwear, a cogent and undeniable comparison. It was also true that the women's swimwear industry in its early stages was closely affiliated with the bra and girdle industry, just as men's wear for swimming was intimately, as it were, connected with the underwear business."[59]

---

[56] Thomas Brooks, *London's Lamentations*, in *The Complete Works of Thomas Brooks*, A. B. Grosart ed. Vol. VI, (Edinburgh, Scotland: The Banner of Truth Trust, 1980), 51, 52.

[57] Romans 12:2.

[58] Lenček and Bosker, *Making Waves*, 33.

[59] Richard Martin and Harold Koda, *Splash! A History of Swimwear*, (New York: Rizzoli International Publications, Inc, 1990), 58.

The reasons for this "suppression" should be obvious: under garments have a blatantly erotic appeal. And American culture, with its "decency" theory of clothing, was not prepared in those days for such a flagrant display of sensuality. Clearly the purpose underlying swimwear design was exposing human anatomy in a more sensual package. This could not be successfully achieved on the streets of the city. But in the name of recreation and especially sports, an amazing *dichotomy of thought* began to permeate our society. At the turn of the century, what was naked and lewd in the city was suddenly perfectly justifiable and permissible at the beach.

This should make the child of God think. This shift from streetwear to underwear as a model certainly can't be defended as a move toward modesty. Moreover, in the name of sports, recreation, and following suit with European fashion, Americans began legitimizing public nakedness.

As one account aptly puts it: "The history of the American swimsuit is the square-inch-by-square-inch story of how skin went public in modern times."[60] It's the drama of how flesh, fabric, technology, and media have engaged the Christian view of modesty in a relentless tug of war down by the seaside. This struggle between concealment and display, fabric and skin, modesty and nakedness is a continuing story of how American society—including many Christians—has shed its clothes in public.

Two questions, then, must be answered: first, why was skin *not* public in America until modern times? The answer here is simple. Our culture in general sprang from a Biblical worldview that included *covering* the body.

The second question is what change in our society put skin on display? The evidence seems to be that Christian morality and its attending modesty, which had previously served as resistance to public nudity, simply caved in to growing public pressure. The voice of God's Word was slowly but surely drowned out by the voice of an increasingly secular media, the

---

60 Lenček and Bosker, *Making Waves*, 91.

fashion industry, and public opinion. Consequently, our culture's basis for modesty eroded, almost to the vanishing point. Let me put it another way: no one held a gun to America's head and said, "Strip or die!" The fashion industry simply said, "This is what the fashionable wear"—and our culture eagerly disrobed.

Furthermore, once swimming attire rid itself of the model and coverage of streetwear, a radical transformation took place. Human anatomy was cast in a bold, provocative new light: because the swimsuit became increasingly brief and tight, it became increasingly erotic. This controversy ignited the fires of discord and debate that raged throughout the early decades of the twentieth century. As the swimsuit shrank, the clamor and disputes increased. While every shifting inch of fabric set off another volley of contention, increasing exposure of more flesh successfully stripped away the resistance to public nudity. It is easy to grasp the reason for the intense heat of this pitched battle: the stakes were *extremely* high. This single garment made it possible to expose and eroticize parts of human anatomy which had previously been concealed. The human body was on display in public in a way previously unthinkable in American culture.

The conflict erupting over swimwear was not simply a matter of taste: the metamorphosis of the bathing suit forced our society to reassess its views of modesty. This was a culture war, a war of worldviews. As a people we shifted from the Biblical view of covering the body to an exhibitionist view of showing off the body. The sad outcome is that our society—including its churches—doffed its robe of Christian modesty and stood proud and naked on the beach.

To illustrate this point, let's chronicle the evolution of America's public undressing during the 1900s:

Women's arms were exposed in the first decade. Though this may seem laughable to some in our day, this was a major shift in thought. Women's arms and shoulders were usually covered in public. This change, however, was just the beginning.

The controversy of body concealment versus body display raged on into the 1920s as legs and backs were progressively bared. Cleavage appeared in the 1930s. In their headlong pursuit for more freedom and maximum exposure, swimwear designers jettisoned the overskirt which had been standard fare for most feminine swimming attire. Both men and women wanted to showcase their tan bodies, so the legal prohibitions which were designed to protect public modesty were regularly challenged and all but discarded. Public resistance barely whimpered, slid its clothes off, and joined the crowd.

A technological tour-de-force took place in the 1930s and 1940s, and a major shift in swimwear design followed. New fiber and fabrics allowed the body beneath to come out. These fabrics made it possible to expose more of the body's curves. The body hidden underneath the bulky old suits of the past was now literally emerging into the light of day.

A two-piece suit first appeared in 1935 on the pages of fashion magazines. This bared a few inches of flesh between its two parts. Though some wore this daring item, it would not really become fashionable until the 1940s.

During the 1940s and 1950s two-piece suits bared the midriff. Also popular was the maillot,[61] which was designed with holes and openings to reveal midriff and sides. The maillot focused on the hips and became tighter. Once again, new fabrics made this possible. Elasticated knits accentuated the curves of the body in a way that was previously impossible. Now the body underneath could be amply exposed, emphasized, and exploited in breathtakingly skintight costumes, while its designers could declare that it was "covered." The maillot inched ever lower on the bosom and crept higher on the leg. Most of the newest suits went strapless. Bared shoulders and skin-tight waistlines and bosoms filled the shoreline like high tide.

During this period when swimming attire focused on the body's curves, men with cameras focused on them too. Models smiled and bared themselves for the media, their bodies adorning virtually every kind of advertisement. Young sirens in

---

[61] pronounced *ma-yo*.

bathing suits became a standard item for American merchandising which marketed everything from automobiles to political campaigns.

The navel was exposed in the 1960s and 1970s. Then in the 1970s high cuts revealed hips. Designers bared women's thighs sometimes to the waist, which bedazzled the America public with yet another erogenous zone. This made the so-called "conservative" one-piece suit more erotic than ever. And with each new fashion season, the creators of swimwear shifted and manipulated the new fabrics to unveil yet another part of the body. Their garments virtually shouted at onlookers, "Look here! Now look there!" And in the 1980s and 1990s even more radical expressions like thongs revealed breasts and buttocks.

The designer's intentions quite obviously were to disrobe and showcase parts of the human anatomy which had never before been "up for grabs" in public. Their constant eroticizing and de-eroticizing portions of the body and their perpetual search for the next erogenous zone to expose screams *design*. A brief look at three of the swimsuit's most famous designers should make this abundantly clear.

Uninterested in his family's business which specialized in making drop-seat underwear, Fred Cole went to Hollywood to become an actor. When this didn't work out, he later joined the family business. Cole's heart was apparently set on crafting swimwear, not long johns. His creative energies were animated by the conviction that a swimsuit was "not so much a garment to swim in but something to look beautiful in."[62] He "dreamed of spectacular women with the velvety eyes and shapely limbs of silent screen actresses. He envisioned them in dramatically cut bathing suits that transformed the body into a living theater of the Id . . ."[63] Driven by this, he designed his first suit with a "deeply scooped front and armholes, low-slung waist, and diminutive skirt above short trunks." The result? "A

[62] Ibid., 51.

[63] Ibid.

dizzying vision of sexuality."[64]

Margit Fellegi, the"crazy Hungarian" from Chicago, regularly challenged the textile industry to create fabrics that would hug the body's curves the way she visualized them. "Her particular genius lay in finding that unexpected approach to the body that made it at once disturbing and seductive . . . Whatever the device, there was always an element of shock in her suits."[65]

Carol Schnurer, a plump and benign woman with graying hair and steel-rimmed glasses, "dedicated her life to persuading other women to take off as many clothes in public a possible."[66] In 1931, she designed, "the forerunner of the two-piece suit. Her own showroom models were so horrified by the unprecedented exposure of bare midriff that they refused to put it on."[67]

Surpassing all others in the fashion industry, swimwear designers have stunningly triumphed in changing public opinion regarding modesty. It is crystal clear that their creations are designed to expose as much human flesh to the public as possible And yet, there remains in our society a few lingering twinges of bashfulness. As one historian notes, "Even today, when the body has become a marketable package, making a public appearance in a bathing suit can be a disquieting experience."[68]

I must raise two questions here: 1) Given that modern swimsuits were designed to promote public nakedness and remain the most revealing form of clothing, why do so many Christians wear them in mixed company and encourage their young people to do so? 2) Why do Christian ministers and leaders expose God's young men and women to the disquieting experience of "greater body exposure" in the name of evangelizing them? As the above authors admit, there is a forced and uneasy alliance between modesty and sexual display. The Bible speaks of *covering* the body; the world promotes *uncovering*

---

[65] Ibid., 76.

[66] Ibid.

[67] Ibid., 76.

[68] Kidwell and Steele, *Men and Women*, 118.

the body. Should preachers of the Gospel of Jesus Christ be involved in promoting sexual display for which our young people would have been *arrested* sixty years ago? The reason that swimsuits can be "disquieting" is because they expose the bodies of those who wear them. Let's face the truth—a bathing suit tells a more honest story about you than any other form of dress. Young women know that other young women and especially young men will really see whether they are full-busted or flat, what their legs and derrieres are shaped like, whether they have chunky or lean thighs, pretty skin, roundness, boxiness - it's all out in the public in swimsuits. Swimwear by design is the classic case of trying to have your cake and eat it too. It was devised to offer nudity *and* covering at the same time. If one wants to see a women with as few clothes on as legally possible, he need look no further than swimwear advertisements. Given the connection between the two, we shouldn't be surprised that these are virtually indistinguishable from underwear advertisements. So if clothing can't be dispensed with altogether, swimwear at least gives the appearance of nudity. That's what it's *designed* to be.

When the new "Molded-fit" swimsuits were introduced in 1933, they were actually touted as the answer to "nude bathing." An advertisement from then raved, "No other human device can even approximate that utter freedom, that perfection of fit, at rest or in motion, that airy but strictly legal sense of wearing nothing at all." This was not written in the 60s nor did it appear in *Playboy* or *Penthouse*—it was *Harper's Bazaar* in *1933!* What I hope the reader will see is that swimwear was intentionally a prime player in America's not-so-subtle slide into public debauchery.

For over 100 years, this single garment has served as the most important vehicle for the public undressing of America. Swimwear manufacturers have been primary players in "drawing the line in the sand" in the culture war between Christian modesty and nakedness. They have set the standards for what is exposed and what is concealed, while neither their standards nor their ethics are drawn from the Word of God. History clearly demonstrates that their vision has often collided violently with the laws of the land; but more importantly, it has also collided violently with the holiness of God.

Sixty years ago, dressing this way was called "indecent exposure." Today some pastors, Sunday School teachers, and Bible conference leaders call it "Christian liberty" and "a thing indifferent." To believe that a garment *designed* to eroticize various parts of the body is a thing indifferent manifests the dichotomy of thought mentioned earlier. Here's what the dichotomy produces: men and women who would never dream of walking out the front door in their undergarments will parade their nearly naked bodies publicly in swimwear. How many of you ladies would stand in your front yard in only your half-slip and bra? Have you considered that they probably cover more than what you wear to the beach? The dichotomy also produces people who sit in church on Sunday decrying public immorality, while remaining unaware that the garment they will wear to the next retreat would have landed them in jail for public nakedness a few decades ago! A woman wearing a so-called "modest" one-piece swim suit today would have been *arrested* in 1922, as newspaper archives reveal.

How did this happen to men and women whose bodies are the temple of the Holy Spirit? Though there is today a resurgence of the doctrines of God's sovereign grace and a renewed cry for holiness, somehow the swimsuit has managed to survive within the professing Christian (and even the Reformed) community. Not only has it survived, but it *thrives* and is actually defended and dignified as a "liberty" for God's people. This is perplexing. However, I shall offer a few suggestions in the chapters to come as to how this came about. Prior to that, however, we will consider the stage on which American Christians have performed their sanctified striptease. As we shall see next, it has truly emerged as a theater of the erotic.

VI

The Theater of Carnality

I made a covenant with mine eyes;
why then should I think upon a maid?
Job 31:1

God created beaches. They are a beautiful part of His creation. The splendor of the sand, waves, and sun reflect the glory of their Maker. Lovely as they are, however, they have become the sad theater in which a fierce battle for modesty was lost. During the latter years of the 19th century and the early years of the 20th, going to the beach nearly evolved into a religion for Americans. Between the media hype that constantly touted "healthy recreation" and the fashion industry's brilliant and strategic success in presenting swimwear as "fashionable," a mental dichotomy developed in the American mind that has not left us: nakedness which was unacceptable on city streets quite literally became high fashion on the beach. The atmosphere of the beach not only justified nakedness, but became a new theater of eroticism whose lure was too intoxicating and seductive for most human beings to ignore. A few pulpits decried the obvious moral outrage of the new mentality; but they were soon silenced, rarely to be heard from again. The rush to the beach opened the door for justifying public nakedness.

This "retreat to the beach" is so deeply entrenched in the American psyche, that many of us are probably unaware that men and women frolicking together in the surf was virtually unknown in human history until the mid-1800s. As the cry for more "functional" swimwear arose, the public's morality slipped right off with its outer garments and was laid aside like an old, empty dress. The beach became the stage on which the main character of a new morality play was purposely, progressively, and provocatively disrobed: the female body.[69]

"For women, the preservation of modesty became a crucial concern during the last three decades of the nineteenth century, when they made the uneasy transition from bathing to swimming . . . by mid-century men, women, and children were escaping to this seasonal world [*the beach*] by the thousands as a retreat from the pressures of urbanization and industrialization, and out of this pleasure culture the "summer girl"was born. She took obvious delight in tantalizing male vacationers with her daring antics and costume . . . As the summer girl and her more conservative followers became the common sight on public and private beaches, bathing developed into a highly social form of coed recreation. Functional bathing clothing was no longer adequate, and women adopted styles that showed off their charms . . . contrary to popular etiquette codes, young men not only refused to avert their eyes but some of the more brazen "Kodak fiends" often gathered at the water's edge to watch these living pictures of 'Venus rising from the Sea.'"[70]

It is obvious that for our culture has become extraordinarily clever at concocting beach "pastimes." Every kind of organization can find some reason for gathering at the beach— from vacations and watersport events to seminars and church retreats. Love for the beach and the "Undressed Life" is so deeply embedded in modern American culture that to question its propriety is thought to be the height of legalistic Pharisaism,

---

[69] Male nudity is dealt with in this article as well; however, the main emphasis will be the female because in our culture the fashion industry understands what the pornography industry does: female nakedness makes more money than its male counterpart.

[70] Kidwell and Steele, *Men and Women*, 119.

a return to Puritanical kill-joyism. Nevertheless, even modern fashion historians rightly observe that "swimming is a social provocation, an edge that may allow for slightly naughty, covertly sensuous behavior. In fact, those who in the nineteenth century saw the beach as a place of indulgence and arid iniquity were not entirely wrong."[71] They also point out the painfully obvious: "The fun-in-the-sun mentality encouraged a heightened sense of body awareness, and women's swimsuits became increasingly more revealing."[72] Body awareness—as if men were not body "aware" enough already! The beach as the "progressive strip show" has veritably streamed towards the real goal of its erotic race: total nudity. In the 1970s, "hair and skin had to be in peak condition, muscles in tone, for exposure in swimwear. The body was in fashion, particularly on the beach, and there was no doubt in anyone's mind that the swimsuit, however delicious, was merely a frame for it . . . all swimwear gradually lost coverage, gained shock appeal, feel appeal, as new soft and shiny fabrics were used . . . but the daring were no longer wearing teeny weeny bikinis: they were removing them at least the top half, on all the leading beaches of the world."[73] This burlesque, of course, could not be acted out in the work place; but the beach provided the ultimate frontier for pioneers willing to brazenly challenge the old morality.

Swimwear not only legitimized nakedness but its Siamese twin, *voyeurism*. The female form was no longer merely a fantasy hidden under layers of cloth and petticoats: it was now a stark, sensual reality for all those who wanted to look. Though righteous Job said, "I made a covenant with my eyes; why then should I think upon a maid?" (Job 31:1), American men established gazing and fantasizing on the "maids" as a red-blooded tradition. "Spectatorship is . . . inherent to swimming . . . what we fail to see in the streets . . . is palpable at the beach . . .

---

[71] Martin and Koda, *Splash!*, 58.

[72] Kidwell and Steele, *Men and Women*, 118-120.

[73] Probert, *Swimwear in Vogue Since 1910*, (New York: Abbeville Press, 1981), 80.

swimwear and spectatorship are indivisible in concept."[74]

If Christians are unaware that the world views the beach this way, they need to wake up. The lost man generally sees the beach as the theater of the body. Do you doubt this? Then consider the following: "If swimwear would ultimately provide the modern imagination with the eroticism of alternatively concealing and revealing the body, the undeniable, first situation of bathing was nakedness . . . People-watching, the great bourgeois voyeurism, is even more interesting when bathing involves an intimate dialogue between clothing and body seldom if ever glimpsed as candidly elsewhere in the spectacle of modern life."[75] In other words, at the beach you can see more of what you cannot legitimately see anywhere else: live, naked flesh. Not only that, it's actually packaged to make it more erotic than most total nudity would be.

Let's face it: packaging is generally far more erotic than raw nudity. Alison Lurie, author of *The Language of Clothes*, observes that "some modern writers believe that the deliberate concealment of certain parts of the body originated not as a way of discouraging sexual interest, but as a clever device for arousing it. According to this view, clothes are the physical equivalent of remarks like "I've got a secret"; they are a tease, a come-on. It is certainly true that parts of the human form considered sexually arousing are often covered in such a way as to exaggerate and draw attention to them."[76] Kidwell and Steele add that "clothes are especially sexy when they call attention to the naked body underneath."[77] Every human being that is even slightly aware of his or her sexuality *knows* this. The same thing applies to short skirts, tight pants, skimpy tops, shorts, and a variety of clothing that conceals and reveals the body underneath. The fashion industry does not believe that the

---

[74] Martin and Koda, *Splash!*, 43, 19, 21.

[75] Ibid.

[76] Lurie, *The Language of Clothes*, 212-214.

[77] Kidwell and Steele, *Men and Women*, 56.

principle purpose of clothing is to cover the body; it believes that the principle purpose of clothing is *sexual attraction*. This is the very opposite of Christian modesty.

It's sad but true: the great dichotomy is alive and well today, and it resides in the minds of a staggering number of pastors and youth leaders. They believe that this arena of legitimized nudity is the ideal place to teach impressionable young men and women the "faith of God's elect, and the acknowledging of the truth which is after godliness" (Titus 1:1). How can this be?

There are many possible explanations for this confusing phenomenon. Time and space will only allow for a few. Some who claim to be men of God are simply unregenerate and will therefore relentlessly fight to clothe fleshly pleasures in the robes of religion. Some professing men of God do not lead—they instead are led by the desires of their people (and particularly by the women and the "youth group"). Others, who are sincere men of God, have so many furious battles in various areas that they simply have not reflected on nor studied the issue. And there are some who have studied the issue over the years and have concluded that this is a thing indifferent, a matter of Christian liberty. Let's take a look at one possibility that might explain why this dichotomy exists in *some* men of God.

VII

The Impact of the Media

I will set no wicked thing before mine eyes Psalm 101:3

How many of today's preachers were "raised on TV?" Pinpoint accuracy might be difficult, but one thing is certain: it's quite difficult to find one that hasn't been influenced by Hollywood, whether he grew up with a TV or not. The Apostle Peter says, "Wherefore gird up the loins of your mind, be sober, and hope to the end for the grace that is to be brought unto you at the revelation of Jesus Christ; As obedient children, not fashioning yourselves according to the former lusts in your ignorance. But as he which hath called you is holy, so be ye holy in all manner of conversation; Because it is written, Be ye holy; for I am holy" (1Pe 1:13-16). Our former lusts all originate in one place: the mind. Sad to say, many good preachers, though commanded to mortify the deeds of the flesh, have tenaciously clutched to the notion that television and movie watching are somehow neutral, and that Hollywood, a major prophet (if not *the* major prophet) of anti-Christian ideology, produces entertainment that must be classed as "Christian liberty." Hollywood is *not* neutral. And exercising *its* liberties, Hollywood discovered in its earliest days that nakedness sells.

> As early as 1914, when Mack Sennett recognized the box-office appeal of parading bathing beauties on the silver screen, the cinema began to carry on a passionate

love affair with the swimsuit. Film stars watched their careers take off like rockets on the strength of publicity shots showing them in swimsuits.[78]

Hollywood's role in undressing America cannot be overstated. Using the new technology of moving pictures, Tinsel Town barraged the American public with increasingly seductive images. This kept the tantalizing threat of public nudity constantly before the eager eyes and minds of our culture. After all, the cinema was an inexpensive form of entertainment during the Depression and drew multitudes into the theaters. Virtually everyone could afford to go to the movies; and because they offered escape from the crushing difficulties of the era, Hollywood emerged as a principle force of fashion styles. Furthermore, its connection with the swimsuit industry was extremely profitable for both parties: "The basic concept, from Jantzen's point of view was, 'I'll sell your movie star, if you sell my bathing suit.' There was no end to the ingenuity of the linkups between the manufacturer and local movie theaters and retail stores . . . The Hollywood connection lent mass-produced suits an enticing cachet of glamour and high style that translated into hefty sales figures."[79]

There was also no end to the ways that Hollywood found to exploit the human body for profit. After all, the body could now be scantily clad, erotically packaged, and projected into dazzling, larger-than-life images for all to see. "[The] erotic bather was being promulgated by swim-wear manufacturers, beauty-pageant promoters, and the Hollywood glamour machine. Submerged chorus lines and splashy synchronized swimming became one of the soft-core pornographies of that decade and the next . . . Hollywood realized that though movies could talk, few conversations equaled the unutterable sex appeal of cinema flesh."[80]

---

[78] Lenček and Bosker, *Making Waves*, 14.

[79] Ibid., 75.

[80] Martin and Koda, *Splash!*, 32, 29.

That Hollywood became a major source of style ideas should be patently obvious, but this has apparently eluded some pastors and youth leaders. The media's impact in selling nakedness to the American public is difficult to exaggerate. Although the printed page once exerted considerable power over men's minds, cinema and television dramatically eclipsed it. What was once simply abstract fantasy in the darkened minds of men became the new reality for this entire nation. The gods of fashion spoke through images on the large and small screens of America and laid hold on its collective imagination like no other media phenomenon in history. Ellen Melinkoff, author of *What We Wore*, reveals the overwhelming influence the new gods of fashion exerted over young women from the 50s to the 80s. Her words epitomize a generation bowing to the voice of Hollywood, not the Word of God:

> When we did like a style, it was often because we were set up to do so by the fashion industry, by television, by fashion magazines, by mothers, by men, by best friends, by the overwhelming examples set by the most popular girls . . . but suburbia and subdebs[81] were minor influences compared with television. TV opened up the world to us, including the fashion world. It let us see what people were wearing with an intensity, and immediacy we had never had. Before that time we relied on *LIFE*, fashion magazines, and movies for guidance. But those media were remote and told us what a model or movie star had worn months ago. With TV, we could see what Dorothy Kilgallen was wearing tonight, what Bess Myerson had on this afternoon, and what Justine and Pat on American Bandstand had worn to their high school this very day.[82]

Melinkoff rightly pinpoints the underlying issue: "we were set up to do so by the fashion industry." The media, especially

---

[81] A girl in her middle teens.

[82] Ellen Melinkoff, *What We Wore: An Offbeat Social History of Women's Clothing, 1950 to 1980*, (New York: William Morrow and Co.), 20, 21.

television, transformed the way young people thought. Because of its powerful and seductive images, idolatry subtly and potently transmogrified from silent images of stone and precious metals into living icons that bared more and more flesh. And America bowed at the altar and submissively followed suit . . . even many of its pulpits.

Nevertheless, the most shameful example of Hollywood's astonishing sway over America's minds was not its seducing women to strip naked, but *men*. The Apostle Paul tells us that Eve was deceived, but that Adam followed her with his eyes open. Like Adam, American males have followed the "Eve" of Hollywood into public nakedness. The following revelation should humble every male reader.

During the 30s "the upper torso became the new focus of concern, and male swimmers who bared their chests in public not only forfeited respectability but faced the penalty of arrest as well . . . the 'nude look' in swimsuits made a mockery of the laws. *Apparel Arts* in 1932 reported that 'many of the bathers of this year . . . swam shirtless, wearing only a pair of Trunks.'"[83] Swimwear designers "fashionably" pressured men to go topless and offered them two-piece swimwear. This "Depression Suit," as it was called, had a removable shirt which could be tucked in, buttoned, or attached to the trunks with a zipper. This was no small contest in the long civil war for modesty: "For nearly three decades, a battle of decency, decision, and decree were fought at the water's edge. In the fourth decade, women's bathing attire changed little in terms of decency, but men's chests became the new field of skirmish . . . Hollywood's men went topless in the 1930s (though airbrushed into the 1950s to avoid the brutality of body hair), and the nation-wide trend, expressing physique while suggesting sensuality, followed with alacrity."[84] In other words, when swimwear designers and their Hollywood connections pressured men into the strip show, they eagerly cast off their tops along with their manhood. Why?

[83] Kidwell and Steele, *Men and Women*, 118.

[84] Martin and Koda, *Splash!*, 29, 43.

Because they followed their hearts instead of God's Word. It's what they wanted.

Guilt for this decaying and debauched state must *not* be laid entirely at the feet of women, as it often is. The problem lies squarely with the men in the pulpits and homes of this nation. With the near dissolution of Christian manhood in this century, American males have become feminized sex-worshipers who do not lead, but are *led*. They have followed their silver-screen icons into nudity, and not the purity of Jesus Christ. Had they followed the God of holiness and governed their hearts and eyes as instructed by God's Word, the present lascivious culture simply would not and could not exist. Nevertheless, any who dare to speak against public nakedness are quickly decried as legalists, Pharisees, and—worst of all— *fundamentalists*. How pathetic that so many pulpits and youth groups today are governed by the desires of the women and children of the congregation and *not* the Word of God. As the Prophet Isaiah said of his day, "This *is* a rebellious people, lying children, children *that* will not hear the law of the LORD: Which say to the seers, See not; and to the prophets, Prophesy not unto us right things, speak unto us smooth things, prophesy deceits" (30:9,10).

Compare what is preached as "liberty" today with Questions 137 through 139 of the Westminster Assembly's *Larger Catechism*:

Q. 137: Which is the seventh commandment ? A. The seventh commandment is, Thou shalt not commit adultery.

Q. 138: What are the duties required in the seventh commandment? A. The duties required in the seventh commandment are, chastity in body, mind, affections, words, and behaviour; and the preservation of it in ourselves and others; watchfulness over the eyes and all the senses; temperance, keeping of chaste company, **modesty in apparel** . . . shunning all occasions of uncleanness, and resisting temptations thereunto.

Q. 139: What are the sins forbidden in the seventh commandment? A. The sins forbidden in the seventh commandment, besides the neglect of the duties required, are adultery, fornication, rape, incest, sodomy, and all unnatural lusts; all unclean imaginations, thoughts, purposes, and affections; all corrupt or filthy communications, or listening thereunto; wanton looks, impudent or light behaviour, **immodest apparel** . . . unchaste company, lascivious songs, books, pictures, dancings, stage plays; and all other provocations to, or acts of uncleanness, either in ourselves or others. (*Emphases added*)

Assuming that the reader believes that the Westminster Assembly was composed of thoughtful, wise Christian men, how would their understanding of Scripture line up with modern Christianity's retreats to the beach? When we expose ourselves to one another in garments designed for sexual attraction, are we honestly *preserving* chastity in body, mind, and affections in ourselves and others? Are we avoiding provocations to sin? Does this really qualify as watchfulness over the eyes and all the senses?

By and large, modern Christians simply don't want these lustful, worldly practices denounced for what they are. Nevertheless, what many Christian males leisurely wear to retreats was considered *indecent exposure* a mere sixty years ago! The laws of this nation declared public swimming in trunks without a shirt to be *nudity*. Even so, the standard practice for Christian leaders is to take our children into an erotic environment and lead them in baring their bodies to one another. And this in the name of bringing them to the holy God!

This present generation has slavishly discipled itself at the feet of Hollywood's effeminate, air-brushed men and has nurtured itself on swimming pools and beach movies. One swimwear chronicle rightly observes that "the real swimsuit show of the 1960s was again realized in Hollywood though not exclusively in publicity shots. A teen-something generation of baby-boomers grew up with movies that took every opportunity to show young bodies in swimsuits, whether in the Hawaiian locales of Elvis Presley films or the beach-blanket high jinx of films featuring Annette Funicello and Frankie Avalon."[85] That "teen-something" generation of men fills a large number of today's pulpits. Since their minds have been shaped by Hollywood's world view and soaked with images of naked male and female forms since they were children, it is not surprising to hear this issue addressed today as "a thing indifferent." Many of us are so desensitized to nakedness that we can look at it and with conviction proclaim, "Liberty!"

Consider these comments about MGM's *Where the Boys Are*: "an innocuous fantasy film about college students on the beaches of Fort Lauderdale, Florida . . . 'sunny, sexy and totally amusing,' the beach party movie developed around an elementary formula of young love, raucous rock 'n roll, and squadrons of bikini-clad starlets . . . the more than 100 beach movies produced during the decade played an important cultural role. Hollywood's rocking beach reels helped establish the world of youth as a separate culture and enshrined the bikini as its official summer uniform . . ."[86] An important cultural role? Yes. These movies helped "enshrine" public nakedness in the hearts of a generation of preachers.

Hollywood has progressively seduced several generations into nakedness and lewdness. What American male or female reading this article *doesn't* have a mind saturated with sensual images of bodies clad in erotic swimwear—images which are permanently seared into the memory by television commercials, magazine ads, billboards, and numerous other media? Tragically for many, these seductive images have further enticed their lustful hearts into the death grip of addiction to pornography. And many of our pulpits remain enshrouded by deathly silence. Or worse, some pulpits cheerily declare that Jesus poured out

[85] Ibid., 113.

[86] Lenček and Bosker, *Making Waves*, 118.

His life's blood upon the cross to purchase us this "liberty." These disciples of the media need to repent of being "conformed to this world" and be "transformed" by the renewing of their minds.

I fear that only the Day of Judgment will fully reveal the extent of the damage wrought by the media upon and through the pulpits of today.

VIII

Candles Among Gunpowder

Love worketh no ill to his neighbour:
therefore love is the fulfilling of the law.
Romans 13:10

We live in a pornographic society. Nevertheless, the children of God are called to purity and holiness. Perhaps because they are drowning in the ecstasy of a sexually debauched culture, some preachers gaze upon its endless parade of sensuality and conclude that swimsuits, short skirts, and other immodest clothing aren't so bad after all. Accordingly, some pastors and youth leaders urge young women to wear "modest, one piece" swimsuits before they lead them to the beach. However, I hope by now it is clear that such a thing is fiction. "People are more body-conscious these days," explained Peggy Gay, a beachwear buyer for Saks Fifth Avenue during the summer of 1977, "and there is a certain sleek sexiness in a one-piece that doesn't exist in a two-piece." [87] This is undeniable. Modern one piece suits are true masterpieces of sensual camouflage, because most women's bodies simply cannot slake the public's thirst for the perfect figure. A one-piece is designed to make the best of "what a woman has." If you doubt that, read your local department store advertisements:

---

[87] Lenček and Bosker, *Making Waves*, 141.

OUR SWIM SHOP IS NOW OPEN

See the difference the right fit can make!

Our Fit Specialists are specially trained and ready to help you determine your correct swimsuit size. They know how to select a suit that really fits through the hips, waist, and bust. And we have a specialist in every store. ___'s takes the guessing out of selecting swimwear. We know that when you are choosing the bare minimum, you want a fit that plays up your assets, not one that calls attention to those less-than-perfect areas . . . on every hang tag, you'll find one or more colored dots to help you find the suit that best flatters your figure.[88]

Bare minimum? Best flatters your figure? What "assets" are you "playing up," ladies? Does this sound like a garment that promotes inner self-government which outwardly displays itself in humility and purity from a genuine love for Jesus Christ? Or is this the very *essence* of self-glorification and self-advertisement? A yard or so of stretchy material that exposes the body underneath is not modest. Does anybody reading this *really* think it is? When virtually every curve of a woman's body is packaged for a sensual public display? A careful study of the literature, images, and photographs from the earliest eras in the evolution of swimwear reveals that controversial zones of the body were progressively laid bare: upper arms and thighs, shoulders and backs. Inching away from the Biblical standard, suits crept up the thigh and down the shoulders to the bosom. Yet for all this daring display, the last sensitive region was for a while still protected: the groin. Throughout the early decades of the 20th century both men and women's suits decently covered this portion of the body. Nevertheless, even this last holdout was unveiled and is now prominently displayed. Most woman's swimsuits sold today clearly define the *mons pubis*.[89] Isn't this clearly *design*? Isn't this

---

[88] Advertisement from a local newspaper

[89] A rounded fleshy protuberance situated over the pubic bones that becomes covered with hair during puberty. Is this not simply another way of "discovering a woman's nakedness"?

the antithesis of Christian modesty? To deny this is to engage in mental gymnastics not befitting a Christian.

Being drawn to a person's God-given beauty is one thing; having one's eyes *directed* to another's body by a sensually designed garment is another. While clothing does not have to smother one's gender, any apparel *designed* to draw the eye to the erotic zones of the body cannot fill the requirement for Biblical decency. The shapes of men and women's bodies are *not* evil; they were designed by a *good* Creator, Who pronounced them *good*. Having said all this, I must make clear that the problem is *not* and never has been swimwear or any other piece of clothing. The problem is *sinful hearts*. Garments, like all material things, are not sinful in and of themselves. But exposing or sensually packaging the body, while provoking lust in others' fallen flesh, is. Advertising agencies learned years ago that decorating virtually *any* product with a scantily clad woman will grab a man's attention. After all, what is the most popular edition of *Sports Illustrated* every year? The swimsuit issue. Does anyone wonder why? Where does your local newspaper advertise "gentleman's clubs" and strip joints? The sports section. Why? Because, while some women are exceptions to the rule, most men *live* in the sports section.

The holy Word of God says that we are not to love the world nor the things of the world (1 John 2:15). Modern swimwear and most of today's fashions are clearly designed for the *world's* standards, not Jesus Christ's. The fashion industry caters to pride, the lust of the flesh, and the lust of the eyes, not purity and holiness. Its purpose is not *covering* the body; but sensually *packaging* or *uncovering* it. The world does not deny this; why then do so many modern Christians? The world seems more honest about this issue than many of the people who fill our churches and our pulpits. America has moved from a worldview that once could say, "The devout Puritan maiden found beauty in prayer and self-discipline rather than in the wearing of pretty clothes and jewelry,"[90] to a worldview that says

---

[90] Daniel Fleischhacker, *Interpretive Costume Design*, (Kalamazoo: New Issues Press, Western Michigan University, 1984), 75.

this about its swimwear: "IT'S *GLAMOROUS* . . . IT'S *EXOTIC* . . . IT'S *DEFINITELY NOT ABOUT SWIMMING*."[91] Men of God, I ask you a question . . . what then *is* it about? Sisters, what *is* it about?

Women should be *especially* aware of how their clothing impacts men; because generally speaking, men are far more visually oriented than women. Richard Baxter wisely commented that women sin when their clothing tends "to the ensnaring of the minds of the beholders in *shameless*,[92] lustful, wanton passions, though you say, you intend it not, it is your sin, that you do that which probably will procure it, yea, that you did not your best to avoid it. And though it be their sin and vanity that is the cause, it is nevertheless your sin to be the unnecessary occasion: for you must consider that you live among diseased souls! And you must not lay a stumbling-block in their way, nor blow up the fire of their lust, nor make your ornaments their snares; but you must walk among sinful persons, as you would do with a candle among straw or gunpowder; or else you may see the flame which you would not foresee, when it is too late to quench it."[93] He goes on to admonish women, saying, "You should rather serve Christ with your apparel, by expressing humility, self-denial, chastity, and sobriety, to draw others to imitate you in good, than to serve the devil, and pride, and lust by it, by drawing men to imitate you in evil."[94] It is quite rare to find a woman who actually understands the affect her clothing has on others. Many truly do not grasp that they are candles among gunpowder.

Likewise, Thomas Manton declared that "garments were given to cover nakedness and the deformity that was introduced by sin; therefore the apostle saith, 'Let the women adorn themselves in modest apparel' . . . the leaving the breasts naked,

---

[91] A world famous catalogue advertising its "perfect swimsuit."

[92] Baxter's original word was *procacious*.

[93] Richard Baxter, *A Christian Directory* in *Baxter's Practical Works* Vol I, (London: George Virtue; reprint ed., Ligonier, Pennsylvania: Soli Deo Gloria Publications, 1990), 392.

[94] Ibid., 393.

in whole or in part, is a transgression of this rule; they uncover their nakedness, which they should veil and hide, especially in God's presence . . . yet usually women come hither with a shameless impudence into the presence of God, men, and angels. This is a practice that neither suits with modesty nor conveniency; nothing can be alleged for it but reasons of pride and wantonness; it feeds your own pride, and provokes lust in others. You would think they were wicked women that should offer others poison to drink.; they do that which is worse, [*they*] lay a snare for the soul; [*they*] uncover that which should be covered . . . Christians should be far from allowing sin in themselves, or provoking it in others."[95]

Manton was addressing those who wore *far* more clothing than today's woman in her short skirts, low-cut blouses, or swimwear. His reasoning is clear and to the point: Christians should be far from provoking sin in themselves and especially others, and sinful nakedness cannot help but do so.

Thomas Brooks also warned that "they that borrowed the fashions of the Egyptians may get their boils and blotches. Certainly such as fear the Lord should go in no apparel, but, *first*, such as they are willing to die in; *secondly*, to appear before the Ancient of Days in . . . *thirdly*, to stand before a judgment-seat."[96]

Our holy Lord Jesus Christ said, "Ye have heard that it was said by them of old time, Thou shalt not commit adultery: But I say unto you, That whosoever looketh on a woman to lust after her hath committed adultery with her already in his heart" (Mat 5:27-28). An obvious point of Jesus' command is that men must guard their hearts and minds by righteously governing their eyes. They are responsible before the living God for how they use them. However, women often don't seem to realize that by this same commandment, *they* are responsible to dress modestly. They are not to dress in sensual, luxurious, or

[95] Thomas Manton, *Sermons upon Titus II: 11-14* in *Manton's Complete Works* Vol.16,(Worthington, Pennsylvania: Maranatha Publications), 138.

[96] Brooks, *London's Lamentations*, 52.

68   *Christian Modesty*

expensive fashions lest they provoke others to sin. Man must answer to God for the way he uses his eyes, while women must be cautious not to cast a stumbling-block before men. David's horrible sin with Bathsheba was clearly *his* fault; yet Bathsheba's unwise and imprudent public nakedness certainly fueled the fires of David's lust: "from the roof he saw a woman washing herself; and the woman *was* very beautiful to look upon" (2 Sam 11:2). Bathsheba failed to govern her modesty; David failed to govern his eyes. Candle . . . gunpowder.

At this point some sisters might object, "But I'm not trying to be sexy or tempting to men!" I trust this is the case. However, despite your best intentions, if you don a stretchy, skin-tight suit *designed* to play up your assets and then expose yourself to the gaze of men, you won't succeed in promoting chastity, no matter how hard you try. Actions speak louder than words; and in this case, Spandex speaks much louder than heart's desire. The same principle applies to short skirts, tight pants, and numerous other garments which expose and advertise the body rather than cover it.

The world and its gods of fashion must not be the standard for how Christians dress, nor must they have the final say on what beauty is. One noted fashion historian writes, "All my research has led me to believe that the concept of beauty is sexual in origin, and the changing ideal of beauty apparently reflects shifting attitudes toward sexual expression."[97] This is the world's standard, but certainly not God's. Regarding feminine beauty the Holy Spirit declares by Solomon, "Favour *is* deceitful, and beauty *is* vain: *but* a woman *that* feareth the LORD, she shall be praised." *This* is the standard. Moreover, women *and* men need to clearly understand that clothes *are* a language, a true *body* language, whether we realize it or not. In light of this, God's children should fervently desire to promote

---

[97] Valerie Steele, *Fashion and Eroticism: Ideals of Feminine Beauty from the Victorian Era to the Jazz Age*, (New York, Oxford: Oxford University Press, 1985), 5.

purity and godly modesty in themselves and those around them.

The saints of God must examine *whatever* they wear and their motives for wearing it by the word of God. The Apostle Paul instructs the church that "whatsoever ye do in word or deed, *do* all in the name of the Lord Jesus" (Col 3:17). Can we honestly and heartily "play up our assets" before the eyes of the Lord Jesus? Paul exhorted the carnal Corinthian church, "Whether therefore ye eat, or drink, or whatsoever ye do, do all to the glory of God" (1Co 10:31). When we "best flatter our figures," can that *possibly* be for glory of God? How we dress must begin with God's glory, not "playing up our assets." Examine your heart, dear reader. Playing up your assets and flattering your figure is more suited to a pornographic society than the society of God's children. You must *always* remember that you live among diseased souls. And, Sisters, you are indeed candles among gunpowder.

IX

THE RETURN TO CHRISTIAN MODESTY

For ye are bought with a price: therefore glorify God in your body,
and in your spirit, which are God's. 1 Corinthians 6:20

Vincent Alsop observed, "That the present generation is
lamentably intoxicated with novelties and as sadly degenerated
from the gravity of former ages, can neither be denied, nor
concealed, nor defended nor, I fear, reformed . . . even 'the
daughters of Zion' have caught the epidemical infection."[98]
Likewise, an epidemic of immodesty infects our churches
today. The principles by which most swimwear fails the
modesty test should be applied to *everything* we wear. We need
to realize that some "coverings" don't really *cover*: tight
clothing brings out the "body underneath" in the same way
swimwear does. While we must not be ashamed of the body
itself as if it were an evil thing, we must properly *cover* it to
preserve chastity of mind and spirit, especially in the corporate
worship of our holy God. Above all, we men must learn how to
govern our hearts and eyes as well as to teach our wives and
children the proper principles of modesty. Although women
are vulnerable to wearing lavish or sensual apparel, their
fathers and husbands are ultimately responsible for what the
women in their homes wear. Christian men *and* women need to

---

[98] Alsop, *Sinfulness*, 490.

study this matter and fervently pray about it, for we truly need a return to a Biblical modesty.

Why *do* we dress the way we do? John Bunyan put the question this way: "Why are they for going with their . . . naked shoulders, and paps hanging out like a cow's bag? Why are they for painting their faces, for stretching out their neck, and for putting of themselves unto all the formalities which proud fancy leads them to? Is it because they would honor God? Because they would adorn the gospel? Because they would beautify religion, and make sinners to fall in love with their own salvation? No, no, it is rather to please their lusts . . . I believe also that Satan has drawn more into the sin of uncleanness by the spangling show of fine clothes, than he could possibly have drawn unto it without them. I wonder what it was that of old was called the attire of a harlot: certainly it could not be more bewitching and tempting than are the garments of many professors this day."[99] The same could be said *today*, dear reader. Examine your own heart. Why *do* you dress the way you do?

The cry of the Feminists is "It's my body, and I'll do what I want." The cry of the modern Evangelical is "It's my liberty, and I'll do what I want." Nevertheless, the declaration of Scripture is this: "What? know ye not that your body is the temple of the Holy Ghost *which is* in you, which ye have of God, and ye are not your own? For ye are bought with a price: therefore glorify God in your body, and in your spirit, which are God's" (1 Corinthians 6:19, 20). You are *not* your own, if you are a Christian. Your whole being—body and soul—is the purchased property of Jesus Christ; and the price paid for *your* body was the breaking of *His*: "This is my body, which is broken for you" (1Corinthians 11:24; Matthew 26:26). Your body belongs to *Him*! He redeemed it with His precious blood on the cross of Calvary. We *must* consider how we adorn His blood-bought property.

---

[99] John Bunyan, *The Life and Death of Mr. Badman*, in *The Works of John Bunyan*, George Offor ed. Vol III, (London: Blackie & Sons, 1875; reprint ed., Grand Rapids, Michigan: Baker Book House Company, 1977), 645.

No doubt, some will cry at this point, "Aaah! But this is *legalism!*" It is *not* legalism to urge God's children to cover themselves, because modesty is the *command* of Scripture. The desire of the regenerate heart is to honor the Lord Jesus and to do whatever brings Him glory by keeping His commandments. "He that hath my commandments, and keepeth them, he it is that loveth me . . . He that loveth me not keepeth not my sayings" (John 14:21, 24). The glory of God and love for Christ should be the primary motives for everything we say, do, and think, which includes what we wear.

I have given you the Scriptures, and I have given you history. And I have taken pains to let the writers of fashion history speak candidly for themselves. I trust that these have provoked you to thought, as well as to love and good works. However, as I mentioned above, if you find the definition of modesty inaccurate or the conclusions in this article unbiblical, then wrestle and pray until the Lord gives you something better. But *pray!* For the love of Christ, *pray!* It is never legalism to call God's children to obey Him according to His Word!

Pray meditating on the very eternal purpose of Almighty God: "For whom he did foreknow, he also did predestinate *to be* conformed to the image of his Son" (Romans 8:29). This earth, this whole universe exists for one reason alone: the God of grace intended to save His people from their sins and make them like His holy Son, Jesus Christ. He poured out His blood on the Cross of Calvary to pay the debt for the sins of His people. By faith in Him alone, their sins are pardoned for all eternity. Christ saves them, cleanses them, and makes them like Himself. And what is *He* like? "Holy, harmless, undefiled, separate from sinners" (Hebrews 7:26).

So then, how shall we properly govern ourselves with regard to this difficult issue? Let's consider these principles: 1) The glory of God must be our primary *aim*—"glorify God in your body" (1 Corinthians 6:20); "*do* all in the name of the Lord Jesus" (Colossians 3:17). 2) Love for Christ must be our *motive*: "We love Him because He first loved us" (1 John 4:19).

3) Remembering that we are the temple of the Holy Spirit and that we are not our own must be our *corrective*. "Your body is the temple of the Holy Ghost *which is* in you . . . and ye are not your own" (1 Corinthians 6:19). 4) Love for others, the preservation of purity in them and us, and the desire not to provoke them to lust will be our *resulting aim*. "Love worketh no ill to his neighbour: therefore love *is* the fulfilling of the law" (Romans 13:10).

May the God of mercy grant us repentance where we have sinned in this matter. Be honest with yourselves and your God, dear reader. Have you ever really given this issue serious consideration? Have any of you brothers or sisters fervently asked the Lord how a holy child of God ought to dress? If not, I urge you to do so with all my heart. Repent of whatever worldliness you find in your hearts. Repent if you dress for the gazes of men and not for the glory of God.

Today many are again valiantly holding forth the Gospel of God's sovereign grace; they are plainly declaring in many quarters the glorious truth of salvation by faith alone through Christ alone. These wonderful, transforming truths should produce a holy, humble, and *modest* people, distinguishable from this lost and dying world. Hence, my fervent prayer is that we ardently love Jesus Christ *and* one another, that we strive together for the unity of the faith, and that we lead lives that magnify the saving grace of our blessed Redeemer. May we live soberly, righteously, and godly in this present world (Titus 2:11-14); and may we never deny these precious truths that we love by clinging to the forms and fashions of this present evil world and its sinful nakedness. Let us glorify God in our bodies, and in our spirits, which are His (1 Corinthians 6:20). And for God's glory and the love of the Lord Jesus Christ, let us return to Christian modesty.

SOURCES ON FASHION:

Changing Styles in Fashion: Who, What, Why, Maggie Pexton Murray

Fashion: the Inside Story, Barbaralee Diamonstein

Fashion and Eroticism: Ideals of Feminine Beauty from the Victorian Era to the Jazz Age Valerie Steele

Fashion from Egypt to the Present Day, Mila Contini

Fashion Power, Jeanette C. Lauer and Robert H. Lauer

Fashion Revivals , Barbara Baines

From Hoop skirts to Nudity, Carrie Hall

Interpretive Costume Design, Daniel Fleischhacker

Making Waves: Swimsuits and the Undressing of America, Lena Lenček and Gideon Bosker

Men and Women: Dressing the Part, Claudia Kidwell and Valerie Steele

Naked We Came, J. Donald Adams

Paris Fashion, Valerie Steele

Splash! A History of Swimwear, Richard Martin and Harold Koda

Swimwear in Vogue: Since 1910, Christina Probert

Taste and Fashion, James Laver

The Language of Clothes, Alison Lurie

The Social Psychology of Clothing, Susan B. Kaiser

What We Wore, Ellen Melinkoff

Women Are Here to Stay, Agnes Rogers